SPOTLIGHT ON
THE
STUARTS

Stewart Ross

SPOTLIGHT ON HISTORY

Cover illustration: Equestrian portrait of Charles I by Van Dyck

Editor: Susannah Foreman
Consultant: Professor I. Roots, Department
of History and Archaeology, University of Exeter

First published in 1987 by Wayland (Publishers) Ltd
61 Western Road, Hove, East Sussex BN3 1JD, England
© Copyright 1987 Wayland (Publishers) Ltd

British Library Cataloguing in Publication Data
Ross, Stewart
Spotlight on the Stuarts.—(Spotlight on history)
1. Great Britain—History—Stuarts,
1603–1714—Juvenile literature
I. Title
941.06   DA375

ISBN 0-85078-974-5

Typeset, printed and bound in the UK at The Bath Press, Avon

CONTENTS

1 THE NEW CENTURY

When Elizabeth I died in 1603, the vast majority of her subjects could not recall the time when she had not been their queen. She had never married and the succession to the throne was disputable. Men laid up 'armour, munitions and victuals' for the trouble that was expected. But to their surprise there was 'no tumult, no contradiction, no disorder' upon the accession of James I, Elizabeth's cousin from the Scottish House of Stuart. Rarely can an era of such change have started so quietly.

At the beginning of the Stuart Age, almost a quarter of a million people lived in London.

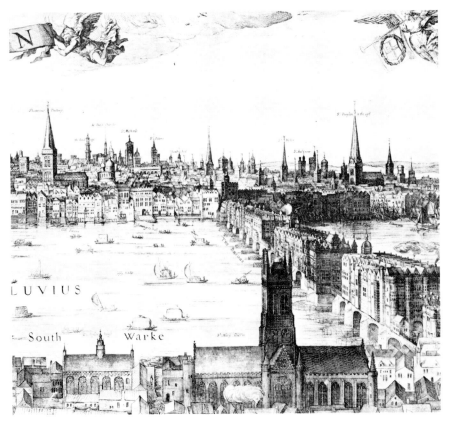

Travel in Stuart England was uncomfortable and slow, with roads little more than stony tracks.

The people

The population of England and Wales in 1603 was about four million and rising rapidly. It had grown by a further million by the middle of the century. Yet compared with the 49 million of today, the country was empty. With the exception of London, where almost a quarter of a million people lived, there were no large cities; Norwich and Bristol had about 15,000 inhabitants, while other towns, such as Exeter or York, could boast no more than about 8,000.

Outside London, only one English person in twenty-five was a town dweller. Most of the population was scattered in small villages and hamlets. When James I arrived in England he complained, 'all the country is gotten into London, so as with time England will only be London and the whole country be left to waste . . .'

Communication in Stuart England was slow. The roads were often broad tracks which sometimes became impassable during winter months. Each parish was responsible for the upkeep of its highways, but this was done inefficiently, even the more conscientious parishes doing little more than fill the larger potholes with stones. Heavy goods had to be shipped by sea and river. There was no regular postal service, and the fastest speed for a message was that of a man on horseback.

With travel difficult and slow, the English identified as closely with the region where they lived as with the country as a whole. The words 'country' and 'county' were interchangeable. During the civil wars (1642–8) armed bands of men stood ready to keep the armies of both sides out of their counties.

Society

The average life expectancy for seventeenth-century Englishmen and women was only just over thirty. The majority of early deaths took place before the age of ten, and a man or woman over the age of fifty was considered old. The reasons for such high mortality were twofold. Firstly, scientific medical knowledge was almost non-existent, as this 1615 cure for the plague shows: '... compel the sick party to sweat, which if he do, keep him moderately therein till the sore begin to rise; then to the same apply a live pigeon cut in two parts ...' A second reason for the short expectation of life was the fact that a high proportion of the population lived below or near the poverty line. Bad harvests, which abounded between 1620 and 1650 when it was 'wonderful wet', brought horrible starvation, malnutrition and death to thousands of the poor and unemployed.

Perhaps 75 per cent of the population were wage earners and craftsmen or beggars and vagabonds, all vulnerable to the ups and downs of the economy. Above them in the social scale was the next largest group, made up of the yeoman farmers, who owned their own land, and wealthier citizens and burgesses of the towns. At the tip of the social pyramid came the royal family, the aristocracy, the knights, gentry and their families, of whom there cannot have been more than about 60,000.

The interior of a cottage in the early 1600s. Most of the population depended on the land for their livelihood.

As this contemporary print shows, the man was very much at the head of the household in Stuart times.

Seventeenth-century England was dominated by men. With a few notable exceptions, the most famous being Queen Elizabeth I herself, women were regarded as second-class citizens. They were expected to obey their husbands and, unless it was financially necessary for them to work, they remained at home. The status of children was even lower. They were often believed to be born wicked and therefore in need of stern discipline to be made virtuous and obedient to their elders and betters. Corporal punishment was widespread.

It is hardly surprising that the privileged classes were obsessed with order. At any moment, they feared, the underprivileged would rise up in revolt. Parliament passed ferocious laws against vagrants, ordering them to be whipped, while in the established Church the congregation were reminded, 'Almighty God hath created and appointed all things in heaven, earth, and water, in a most excellent and perfect order . . . Every degree of people in their vocation calling and office hath appointed to them their duty and order: some are in high degree, some are in low, some kings and princes, some inferiors and subjects . . . so that in all things is to be lauded and praised the goodly order of God.'

The economy

'The soil is fruitful and abounds with cattle', wrote a German visitor to England towards the end of the sixteenth century. 'There are many hills ... which produce a very short and tender grass, and supply plenty of food to sheep.' As we have seen, England was a predominantly agricultural land, whose major industry, wool, was farm based.

The population rise in the first half of the seventeenth century placed considerable pressure upon farmers to produce more food. In some areas, especially in the north, marginal land was taken back into cultivation. Large areas of the fens in East Anglia were drained during the reign of Charles I, and the more business-minded farmers experimented with new techniques, such as manuring fields or growing clover. In some areas broad open fields were divided up with hedges and fences into more manageable units, a process called enclosure. In good years the country could be fed.

Woollen cloth was the only major English manufacture. Hardly a home was without a spinning wheel, for cloth was made in private houses and then collected by merchants for distribution. Cloth was the country's biggest export, and large regions, notably the south-west, East Anglia and West Yorkshire, were dependent upon their exports to the markets of Europe. It is no coincidence that even today our language is peppered with phrases and words drawn from the country's main industry: 'spin a yarn', 'homespun', 'spinster'.

Woollen cloth was England's major industry. The task of shearing sheep by hand was both skilled and laborious.

The village blacksmith was one of the most important members of the community, because of the growing importance of iron.

Besides the woollen cloth industry other branches of English industry were small. Coal was beginning to be mined in some quantity, while iron manufacture flourished in areas where the ore coincided with a plentiful supply of timber for the furnaces. Soap-making, brewing, ship building and a whole host of other industries were small-scale but sufficient to meet the nation's needs. Moreover, following the pioneering work of Elizabethan sailors and merchants, English vessels were becoming more common in the ports of the New World and the old. Although there was no real indication of the country's future commercial importance, James I inherited a realm whose economic prospects were not to be scorned.

2 THE EARLY STUARTS 1603–1642

Most historians no longer regard 1603 as a date of particular significance in English history. The House of Stuart replaced the House of Tudor as the ruling dynasty, but in most respects the government continued much as before. There was little early indication of the troubles that lay ahead.

Stuart government

At the heart of Stuart government lay a paradox. In theory the king could control all administration and all policy, as James I reminded

The House of Commons in 1621. At this time most MPs were more concerned with local matters than national politics.

There were several legal systems in the seventeenth century. Here a man appears before a king's bailiff while another seems to be holding out his hand for a bribe.

Parliament in 1610, 'The State of monarchy is the supremest thing upon earth; for kings are not only God's lieutenants upon earth, and sit upon God's throne, but even by God himself they are called gods.' James believed that God had placed him upon the thrones of England and Scotland. The vast majority of the king's subjects, however, had almost no contact at all with royal government; to them the important powers were at local level: the unpaid Lord Lieutenants or Sheriffs of the county, the magistrates, parish churchwardens or village high constables.

James, like Elizabeth, appointed officials such as the Lord Lieutenants (responsible for organizing the county militia, an armed defence force), from powerful local families. Such people depended upon the Crown for their positions, but at the same time the Crown also depended upon their loyalty and support. The king had no standing army and was always short of money, so in a very real sense the system of government which James inherited was a partnership between the Crown and the upper classes, or 'political nation'. As long as their interests more or less coincided, the system worked.

The Crown and the political nation had two meeting points, court and Parliament. Royal government was exercised by the king and a small group of ministers who formed the Privy Council, but he also held a lavish court where the ambitious sought to catch the king's eye and ear. Powerful figures drew groups of followers around them; hostility between these factions could become very bitter with important political effects.

Parliament, consisting of the Monarch, Lords and Commons, met irregularly, when summoned by the king. Most of its time was taken up with local matters, but in two areas it had considerable potential power: all extraordinary tax had to have the approval of Parliament, and new laws, or acts, also needed its approval.

James I of England. In recent years historians have regarded this intelligent and peace-loving man in a more favourable light.

An engraving showing Puritans reading the Bible. Some religious sects interpreted the Bible in ways that angered the authorities of the Church of England.

James I and VI

In recent years there has been a major revision of our opinion of James I (James VI of Scotland). Historians used to emphasize his physical feebleness, his crude manners and his tendency to lecture his subjects. They quoted freely from James's critical contemporaries: 'his love for favourites is indiscreet and wilful and takes no account of the wishes of his people', and 'his beard was very thin: his tongue too large for his mouth, which ever made him speak full in the mouth.' Today we are more tolerant of James and we realize that he coped successfully with the majority of problems that faced him.

As a Scot, James was seen as a foreigner. The English were suspicious of his alien speech and strange favourites, and he took a while to grasp the intricacies of English government. Nevertheless, in 1604 he wisely ended the expensive war with Spain, which had been dragging on for years, and kept the country officially at peace for the rest of his reign, despite great pressures to involve it in continental war. The Church of England, created by Elizabeth, was still a frail plant. Enthusiastic Protestants, known as Puritans, wished to see it pruned to eradicate any remaining traces of Catholicism, such as bishops, while some Catholics still hoped to see England return to the

17

Roman Catholic faith. The gunpowder plot of 1605 was one of the more famous conspiracies of a papist faction who plotted to blow up James and Parliament at Westminster. The plot failed and the conspirators were executed, but its effects were to increase still further the suspicion and hatred between Protestants and Roman Catholics.

In his handling of Parliament James showed some skill, although towards the end of his reign he allowed the assembly to become a battleground for rival court factions, and he was not always tactful in his approach. Nevertheless, Parliament was not a constant source of opposition to the king, whose most serious problem was finance.

James was supposed to 'live of his own'. In other words, the king was expected to have enough money to run the country from the traditional customs levies, together with the income from royal estates. However, a century of inflation and profligacy had reduced the value of the royal income, rendering it hardly sufficient to meet everyday needs. It proved hopelessly inadequate when the government had to undertake extraordinary expenditure, such as war. The situation was made considerably worse by James's wild extravagance: £68,000 of gifts in the first four years of his reign, when he had a debt of £$\frac{1}{2}$ million and an ordinary income of about £300,000. Successive Lord Treasurers wrestled with the problem, to little effect: by the time of James's death the royal debt had risen to £1 million. Worse still, the hopelessly under-taxed political nation, the only group of people with the power to rectify the situation, could not or would not recognize the seriousness of the problem.

Guy Fawkes, one of the conspirators in the Gunpowder Plot, laying the powder beneath the Houses of Parliament.

Charles I, who was executed in 1649 by Parliamentary rebels, had few of the qualities of leadership necessary for a successful seventeenth-century monarch.

The road to war

Charles I was a short man with a stutter who was almost totally lacking in political skill, and prone to cover his inadequacies with a frosty haughtiness. Such a man was in no way suited to govern the rough and volatile England of the seventeenth century.

Between 1625 and 1629 Charles's government drifted into mounting crisis as it involved the country in wars with France and Spain. Royal forces suffered a humiliating defeat on the île de Rhé, off La Rochelle. The king's favourite, the Duke of Buckingham, was assassinated in 1628 amid increasing grumbling from the political nation in Parliament about the levy of forced loans and the incompetent handling of the war. Charles was even forced to sign a Petition of Right before the House of Commons would vote him further funds.

In 1629 the harrassed king made peace and determined not to call Parliament again. For eleven years the kingdom was governed with

George Villiers, Duke of Buckingham, favourite of James I, with his family. He was assassinated in 1628 because it was felt he had too much sway over the King.

A woodcut of 1648 showing a Scotsman petitioning Charles I about the disturbances caused by the civil wars in Scotland.

some skill, particularly by the able Thomas Wentworth, Earl of Strafford, in Ireland. Charles, however, guided by William Laud, his Archbishop of Canterbury since 1633, made a fatal error: he sought to tighten up on the government of the Church of England and to extend these reforms to the Church in Scotland. The Scots would have none of it. They rose in revolt and marched into England, where resistance melted away. To keep the Scots at bay the king needed money and so, after a false start earlier in the year, in November 1640 there sat for the first time what became known as the Long Parliament.

To begin with, as petition and counter-petition flooded in from the counties, there was considerable unanimity among MPs and peers about what should be done. Wentworth was executed and some of the king's ancient medieval powers were done away with. But how far should the reforms go? And what should be done about the Church? As 1641 drew to a close, with ghastly stories circulating of revolt and massacre in Ireland, two sides began to emerge. By the late summer of 1642 the gap between the king and those in Parliament who opposed him had become unbridgeable. Both sides prepared for war.

3 War and Revolution 1642–1688

By 1640 the system of government built up in the sixteenth century by the Tudors had collapsed. For the next forty-nine years the country struggled to find an alternative as it moved from republicanism to attempted absolutism. The compromise which began to emerge in 1689 was a unique blend of monarchy and parliamentary control, which became the basis of Britain's greatest contribution to the modern world: representative parliamentary government. Although historians disagree as to when the vital change took place, the difference from the early part of the century was a dramatic, irreversible one, and is thus justly termed the English Revolution.

A woodcut published in 1640 depicting the world turned upside down by the outbreak of Civil War.

A satirical view of the two sides in the Civil War: the Cavaliers, and their opponents, who fought for Parliament, the Roundheads.

Civil War

The Civil War which broke out in 1642 was not welcomed by the majority of Englishmen and women. Only with reluctance did soldiers join either side and for much of the war the armies were small and amateurish. Most people, finding themselves 'at the pit's brink, ready to plunge ourselves into an ocean of troubles and miseries', drew back, and hoped that they would not get pulled into the struggle.

Those who were prepared to fight for the king tended to be found in the more northern and western parts of the country, men such as Sir Edmund Verney who wrote in 1642: 'I have eaten [the king's] ... bread and served him near thirty years, and will not do so base a thing as to forsake him.' On the royalist side were those who favoured the older ways, were suspicious of Puritan ambitions, and who favoured the Church of England. The Parliamentary side attracted Puritans, those who had suffered at the hands of arbitrary Stuart government, and idealists who hoped for a more representative system of government. Parliament's strength lay in the south and east, in the towns, and particularly in London.

After two years of indecisive fighting, during which royalist moves towards London were beaten off, Parliament reorganized its army and appointed new competent commanders, Sir Thomas Fairfax and Oliver Cromwell. At the battles of Marston Moor (1644) and Naseby (1645) the royalist armies were smashed. Not only had Parliament developed a more competent army but it also had the support of an effective Scottish force, the backing of the navy and considerably greater economic resources. Charles I now had to negotiate.

During the years 1645–9 the situation in England grew increasingly confused. Charles refused to keep any agreement with his vanquishers, whom he regarded as mere rebels. The Scots wished to have some say in the way events shaped in England, while the Parliamentary forces split into different groups and factions, on religious and political lines. Faced with the possibility of anarchy, and supported by the army (the only effective force remaining), Oliver Cromwell found himself compelled to act. A second civil war was won, London seized and finally, after a show trial, Charles I was executed in 1649. The gesture was dramatic and final. But had it solved anything?

The interregnum
For eleven years Britain was ruled as a republic. In many ways the achievements of this period were remarkable. Using the power of Parliament's New Model Army, Oliver Cromwell subdued the Scots

The crucial battle of Marston Moor (1644) at which the Cavaliers, led by Prince Rupert, were soundly defeated by Cromwell's forces.

The execution of Charles I in 1649 did little to solve the problems that had caused the Civil War.

and restored English rule to Ireland. For the first time the three countries came under the same central and relatively efficient administration. The armed forces also restored English prestige abroad. Between 1652 and 1654 a successful war was fought against the Dutch, Britain's greatest commercial rival. Towards the end of the decade, in alliance with France, English forces captured Spanish territory in the Caribbean and in 1658 helped to defeat the Spanish soundly at the battle of the Dunes near Dunkirk. With some exaggeration a Venetian diplomat wrote in 1655 that 'the Court of England by sheer force had made itself the most dreaded and most conspicuous in the world.'

During the interregnum the country witnessed a freer economic climate, some religious toleration and more efficient local government. Yet few long-term problems were solved and after the death of Cromwell in 1658 the republic had only about another eighteen months to live.

Following the execution of Charles I in 1649, the remainder of the Long Parliament, known as the Rump, governed the country through a Council of State. The Council promised much but achieved little and in 1653, with the unflinching support of the army, Cromwell drove out the Rump and set up a nominated Assembly of godly people of his and others' choice. Upon the failure of this 'Parliament of Saints' a few

Oliver Cromwell, backed by his army, dissolved the Long Parliament in 1653. The Parliament had first met in November, 1640.

months later, Cromwell accepted the title Lord Protector, under which guise he governed the country until his death. He summoned two Parliaments, with both of which he quarrelled, just as Charles I might have done, although the second one offered him a crown, which he rejected. Thus, when Oliver's son Richard proved unwilling and unable to take up his father's mantle, following a period of mounting chaos, the political nation turned once again to the only form of government truly familiar to them: monarchy. On 25 May 1660, Charles I's elder son stepped ashore at Dover. A short while later, amid widespread rejoicing, he was crowned Charles II.

Charles II

Charles II was a very different character from his father. Intelligent and quick-witted, he was also lazy and wholly lacking in principle. Having spent a good part of his early life in uncomfortable exile, the one fixed point in his policy seemed to be a determination 'never to go on his travels again.' The skilful terms upon which he was restored in 1660, based upon a document called the Declaration of Breda which Charles issued from Holland, did nothing to solve the deep-rooted difficulties which had beset the English constitution since 1625. Before long, Charles was facing problems similar to those which had confronted his father.

By a series of laws known as the Clarendon Code, after Charles's first chief minister, the Earl of Clarendon, the Church of England was

26

restored and the activities of those who could not accept it—the dissenters—were severely limited. The king retained the right to choose ministers and make policy, but he was short of money. His income constantly fell short of the £1.3 million that Parliament had intended he should receive in 1660, and so until almost the end of his reign he was dependent upon Parliament for extra grants and taxes. In return, of course, Parliament expected some say in what the money was to be used for.

The early part of Charles's reign witnessed two further commercial wars against the Dutch (1664–7 and 1672–4) and growing suspicion of Charles's friendship with the most powerful monarch in Europe, the Catholic Louis XIV of France. Men were worried lest the heir to the throne, Charles's Roman Catholic brother James, Duke of York, try to emulate Louis when he became king. There was a move to exclude James from the succession, and several times an Exclusion Bill came close to getting through Parliament: 'It is enacted that James, Duke of York, shall be and is by the authority of this present Parliament excluded and made forever incapable to inherit or enjoy the imperial Crown.' However, owing to Charles's skill and the mistakes of his opponents, the Whigs, the exclusion movement collapsed in 1681, and over the last four years of his reign Charles took several steps to strengthen the Tories, those loyal to his brother and the Crown's traditional powers. It remained to be seen what James would do with this not unpromising inheritance.

The coronation of Charles II. After years in exile, Charles returned to England in 1660 determined never to leave the country again.

In the middle of the century there were three Anglo-Dutch wars, fought largely for commercial reasons.

4 THE CHURCH AND ITS OPPONENTS

'Let them chant while they will of prerogatives', wrote the seventeenth-century Puritan poet John Milton, 'we shall tell them of Scripture; of custom, we of Scripture; of Acts and Statutes, still of Scripture ...' Religion, as Milton explains so forcefully, was not just an aspect of life in the seventeenth century; for most men and women it was an essential part of everything they did. Science, politics, literature, the weather, medicine—in all areas of life religion played a prominent part.

The Church of England

Until the early sixteenth century all western Europe had belonged to the Roman Catholic Church. Then, during a long and complicated movement called the Reformation, many groups known collectively as Protestants broke away from the Catholic faith and established their own churches. Protestant groups differed, but on a few basic beliefs they were in agreement: they rejected the authority of the pope, permitted priests to marry, translated the Bible from Latin into the vernacular, and replaced the elaborate mass with more simple communion or remembrance services.

England broke with Rome between 1529 and 1535, during the reign of Henry VIII. Briefly, during the reign of Henry's daughter Mary (1553–8) the country reverted to Catholicism before Elizabeth re-established the Church of England in 1559.

The English Church was in many ways a compromise. Its services were in English and its priests married, but the ancient Catholic hierarchy of archbishops, bishops, archdeacons and clergy, abandoned by other Protestants, was retained. This was because the Queen, the Supreme Governor of the Church, wished it so. The Church, with its network of pulpits and near-monopoly of education, was a vital weapon for the control of opinion and for the spreading of information. The clergy were in effect expected to be unpaid royal servants.

When James I came to the throne Anglican practices had filtered through to most English communities, although there were parts of Wales and the north where Catholicism would linger on. James did what he could to create a learned, able clergy, but the extreme

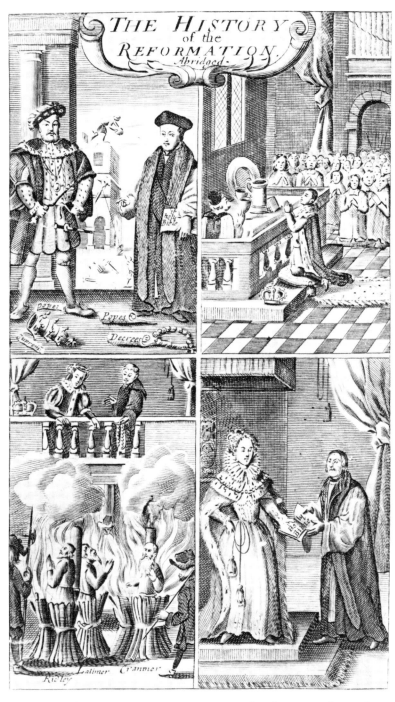

During the Reformation Protestant groups broke away from the Catholic faith and established their own Churches.

Anglicanism of Archbishop Laud, which to many looked like Roman Catholicism in disguise, was a major factor in the collapse of royal government in 1640. During the interregnum the Church of England was persecuted and despoiled, but returned 'lock, stock and barrel' in 1660–65. In the eyes of the political nation the Church of England was now part of the political establishment and its status was reinforced by harsh laws, such as the 1662 Act of Uniformity. A link was thus forged between the vicar and the squire which was to survive until well into the nineteeth century.

The Puritans

There is no satisfactory definition of a Puritan. One contemporary described them as 'the hotter sort of Protestants' and that is possibly as good a definition as any. The term Puritan was used of all sorts of groups, but essentially it applied to those enthusiastically-religious people who wished to see the Church of England purified of its remaining Roman Catholic elements. Thus many Puritans objected to the institution of bishops, to the communion table being railed off and termed an altar, to elaborate ceremony, rich priestly clothing and church decoration. They complained bitterly that the clergy preached insufficient sermons to spread the word and educate the laity.

Leaders of the Anglican Church wanted to ensure that travelling preachers were licenced and taught only orthodox doctrines.

Since the monarch was at the head of the Church of England, to criticize the Church was to criticize part of the royal authority, so Puritanism was frowned upon by the Stuart monarchs. James I wisely did not press his mistrust too hard, but his son was more vigorous. Archbishop Laud spoke thus of the bishops, at a famous trial of Puritan preachers: 'No man can libel against our calling, be it in the pulpit or in print, but he libels against the King and the State by whose laws we were established.' Yet in the eyes of the Puritans the bishops were merely 'those little toes of Antichrist'.

With the defeat of the king in the civil war, the Puritans came to power. One of their more extreme gestures was to abolish Christmas as a pagan festival, but most people would have noticed more readily the simplified services and destruction of church ornaments, such as stained-glass windows.

In 1660 it was accepted that Puritanism would survive, but only Anglicans were allowed political rights. The Puritans, who are now generally referred to as Nonconformists or Dissenters for their unwillingness to conform to the 1660 religious settlement, finally received a measure of toleration in the 1689 Toleration Act. Gradually, from this time onwards the bitterness associated with religious differences subsided, but even to this day the Church of England remains the only official established Church in Britain.

A satirical print of a Puritan, showing him to be excessively pious.

Mary I (1553–8), whose persecution of Protestants did much to establish later hatred of Catholicism.

Catholicism

For most of the seventeenth century the term Catholic was associated with the most evil acts. In the reign of Mary I 300 English Protestants had been burned at the stake, many in London's Smithfield. This persecution became imprinted on the minds of all Englishmen in the best seller of the day, John Foxe's *Acts and Monuments*. Thereafter there was hardly a plot, a murder, a disaster but Catholics were suspected. These widespread fears were reinforced by real Catholic danger in the form of the Spanish armada of 1588, the Gunpowder Plot of 1605 and the Irish revolt of 1641. As late as 1679, at the time of great fear of a popish plot, the Earl of Essex confessed, 'the apprehension of popery makes me imagine I see my children frying in Smithfield.'

The politics of the seventeenth century are incomprehensible without recognizing the power of anti-Catholic sentiment. With the exception of the Dutch, the country's wars were fought against Catholic states, Spain and France, whose absolutist regimes were supposed to epitomize the tyranny of the 'dregs of Rome'.

In reality the number of Roman Catholics living in Stuart England was small (perhaps only 35,000 in 1603) and the great majority were law-abiding, honest citizens. Although in theory they were subject to strict fines, in practice they were left unmolested for much of the time if the local magnate was either Catholic or had Catholic sympathies. For much of the century the most powerful Catholic patrons were to be found at court, a fact which frightened and bewildered so many subjects. Both James I and Charles I had Catholic wives who were permitted their own priests and services. Charles II's wife, Catherine of Braganza, was a Catholic, and Charles himself died a confessed papist. His brother, James II, lost his throne largely because of his tactless advocacy of Roman Catholicism.

The burning of Bishop Hooper in 1555 was included in John Foxe's Book of Martyrs, *a book widely read in the seventeenth century.*

Charles II's Roman Catholic Portuguese wife, Catherine of Braganza, brought the ports of Tangiers and Bombay as part of her dowry.

Anti-Catholic feeling was strong, as this contemporary satire shows, with the Pope on high, while Jesus is in the stable.

Toleration

During the seventeenth century there was a gradual acceptance that religious toleration was not an automatic recipe for chaos and revolution. This was never officially extended to any but Protestant sects but, as we have seen, in practice Roman Catholics were left to worship in peace for much of the time. What the spread of toleration in fact meant was that the Church of England had failed to become the Church of all the people in the way that the old Roman Catholic Church had before the Reformation. Many had striven to create a 'comprehensive' Anglican Church, particularly Charles II and Clarendon. The 1689 Toleration Act marked the failure of such attempts: '. . . as some ease to scrupulous consciences in the exercise of religion may be an effectual means to unite their Majesties Protestant subjects in interest and affection.'

To some extent toleration had been granted statutorily to the Nonconformists in 1689 because they had sided with Anglicans in their opposition to the Catholic absolutist designs of James II: in the eyes of the ruling class, toleration was their reward. But toleration had other roots. By the late seventeenth century the intellectual climate was beginning to change.

Since the sixteenth century there had been under way a remarkable alteration in thinking, which we now call the Scientific Revolution. Its hallmark was the application of experiment and reason to the understanding of the world. The scientists, among whom were the creative Robert Boyle (1627–1691), Robert Hooke (1635–1703) and, above all, Sir Isaac Newton (1642–1727), did not accept inherited truths. Instead, they experimented and researched before coming up with the most likely hypotheses. Newton, as well as being interested in alchemy, was a sincere Christian all his life, but the rational methods which he utilized and popularized belonged to a different world from the fiery fanaticism of the pamphlet of 1679 which warned, 'whenever Popery prevails: imagine you see the whole town aflame ... behold troops of Papists ravishing your wives and daughters, dashing your little children's brains out against the walls ... imagine your father and mother tied to a stake in the midst of flames ...'.

Sir Isaac Newton (1642–1727) is the best known among the many celebrated seventeenth-century men of science.

5 FOREIGN AFFAIRS

When James VI of Scotland ascended the English throne in 1603 he acquired a country larger, more populous, more sophisticated and vastly more wealthy than his native Scotland. Yet England herself at the opening of the seventeenth century was scarcely more than a minor power on the fringes of European affairs. However, by the death in 1714 of the last Stuart monarch, Anne, the situation had dramatically altered, as had the whole balance of power within Europe.

Scotland

It is important to remember that in the seventeenth century the English regarded Scotland as a foreign country. Although James I and VI united the crowns of England and Scotland, that was as far as the unity went and his attempt at further union was rudely thwarted by the English Parliament in 1607. This is hardly surprising given the ridiculously hostile attitude of the English towards the Scots: 'To be chained in marriage with one of them, were to be tied to a dead carcase, and cast into a stinking ditch.'

After Charles I's failure to impose Laud's church reforms on the Scots, that country entered upon a period of considerable instability before being subdued by Cromwell's troops and forced to accept union with England in 1654. The kingdoms were separated again at the Restoration but well before the end of the century union was once again in people's minds. The English feared that supporters of the exiled James II and his son (the Old Pretender, self-styled James III) would always find sympathetic support in Scotland, while the Scots looked longingly at their southern neighbour's dramatic commercial and economic progress. The 1707 Act of Union, although unpopular in some circles, proved the obvious answer in the long run. The Scottish economy blossomed while the English received peace of mind, and a steady flow southwards of Scottish talent.

Ireland

The story of Ireland in the seventeenth century is a tragic one. As the century opened the English were in the process of crushing a long-lasting Spanish-aided Catholic revolt against their overlordship. By 1604 resistance was ended. There now followed a policy of 'plantation' by which English and Scottish Protestant settlers were given favourable terms to colonize Ireland, particularly in the north. The island,

James II's son, although spending almost all of his life in exile, styled himself James III, but was known as the Old Pretender in England.

whose inhabitants were regarded by the English as semi-human barbarians ('bog trotters'), now had an alien governing class.

Following the harsh but efficient Lord Deputyship (1632–40) of Thomas Wentworth, Earl of Strafford, Ireland rose in revolt against her foreign overlords, only to be crushed by Cromwell's New Model Army between 1649 and 1650. In order to cow the population, on his arrival

When Cromwell took Drogheda in 1649, he massacred many of the Catholic Irish defenders, whom he regarded as barbarians.

Thomas Wentworth, Earl of Strafford, was Charles I's ablest advisor. Parliamentarians secured his execution in 1641.

Cromwell ruthlessly destroyed the garrisons of Drogheda and Wexford, burning some rebels in the steeple of a church where they had taken refuge, and as for the others, 'when they submitted, their officers were knocked on the head, and every tenth man of soldiers killed, and the rest shipped for the Barbadoes ... I am persuaded', continued Cromwell, 'that this is the righteous judgement of God upon these barbarous wretches.'

A final upsurge of Irish nationalism occurred towards the end of the century. The exiled James II landed there in 1689 and inspired his co-religionists to join him in an attempt to wrest back his throne. For a while 'Ireland was again a nation' and Protestant forces were beseiged in the fortifications of the north and east. But William III's forces were too strong. At the Battle of the Boyne (1690) James was defeated and soon fled back to France, leaving Ireland to slow reconquest and further long years of colonial subservience and oppression; with repercussions continuing into our own times.

James II's attempt to retake the thrones of England and Scotland was defeated at the Battle of the Boyne, 1690.

England and Europe

England's traditional relations with Europe had been dominated by two things, fear of invasion and the wool and cloth trade. For centuries England's wealth had depended upon her export of fine wool and, more recently, unfinished cloth to the markets of Europe. This necessitated friendship with the powers controlling the major ports of the Low Countries. Fear of invasion also invited similar friendships and invariably led to tension with Britain's old enemy, France.

During the reign of Elizabeth England's foreign policy underwent a revolution. With France beset by civil war, Protestant Europe was threatened by Spanish Catholic domination. Both the Dutch and the English fought for national survival, and were also tempted to pirate Spanish wealth in the New World. King James, realizing that, for financial reasons, his government was incapable of fighting a major war, saw himself as arbiter of Catholic and Protestant Europe, *Rex Pacificus*. His son's two brief conflicts in the late 1620s were of little long-term significance, and after 1629 he too was in no position to play a direct part in the European war raging at the time, although English people could not be entirely indifferent to it.

By the middle of the century the pattern of European power was changing again. Spain, although still wealthy and influential, was in decline. Holland had emerged as a major commercial force, while a reinvigorated and more centralized France was swiftly developing as the most powerful country in Europe. Three times the English fought the Dutch in commercial wars (1652–4, 1664–7, 1672–4) and Cromwell took advantage of Spain's weakness to plunder her Empire. But by the time of the last Dutch war there was general unease at two small Protestant nations warring, while mighty Catholic France looked on and took advantage.

With the accession of the Dutchman, William III, whose nation was threatened with extinction at the hands of the French, English fears were translated into action. The last decades of the Stuart era were largely taken up with wars against France. In the reign of Anne (1702–14) allied armies under the command of John Churchill, Duke of Marlborough (1650–1722) brought England greater European influence than she had enjoyed since the reign of Henry V, almost 300 years before.

John Churchill, Duke of Marlborough, who won four resounding victories over the armies of Louis XIV of France in the early 1700s.

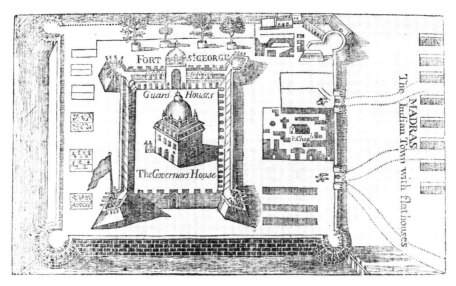

Fort St George, Madras, was founded by the East India Company in 1639. From small posts like this the company went on eventually to control almost the whole Indian sub-continent.

Empire

There was little indication in the first half of the seventeenth century that England would become a major colonial and commercial power in the course of the next century. The Dutch dominated European trade, and Amsterdam was the continent's major entrepôt. English merchants did take more of the nation's trade into their own hands, however, and commercial links were spread more widely, notably into the Mediterranean. Nevertheless, serious trade slumps in 1614–17, 1621–4 and 1640–2 fixed a pattern of cautious, unspectacular development.

The same was true of England's colonial development. The first colony was settled in 1607, at Jamestown in Virginia, North America. After three tough years it was described 'rather as the ruins of some ancient fortification, than that any people living might now inhabit it. The pallisadoes ... torn down, the ports open, the gates from the hinges. The church ruined and unfrequented ...'. Yet the colony survived. Others followed in Virginia and Maryland, on Caribbean islands, and in the area called New England (Plymouth, Massachusetts). By 1650 the total colonial population was about 50,000.

From the middle of the century a commercial revolution began. Although it is dealt with in more detail later, it is worth noting here that it found its heart in colonial trade. By 1700 the population of the Caribbean and American colonies was approaching half a million. To the original colonies were added New York, the Carolinas, Pennsylvania and New Jersey, as well as Jamaica, Barbados, Antigua and other West Indian islands. In the East the East India Company built up Bombay as a major trading post. The foundations of the British Empire had been laid.

6 THE LATER STUARTS 1688–1714

Following the revolutions of 1688–9, the reigns of the last Stuarts mark a period of settling and healing in English politics. They also witnessed expansion in the commercial and industrial life of the nation. Although the country was at war for much of the period, it prospered and the taxation needed to finance the costly wars against Louis XIV's France, instead of alienating the political nation from the government, served rather to bind it more closely to the regime which it had brought about.

Although James II was a Catholic, people were prepared to accept this as he had no male heir. Views changed after the birth of his son in 1688.

The Glorious Revolution

James II inherited several of his father's unfortunate characteristics. Above all, he seemed incapable of tempering his policies to match the wishes of his people. In three brief years he undid all his brother's careful work in building up royal authority, and at length he felt compelled to flee abroad, leaving the kingdom to his daughter and her Dutch husband.

James used relatively obscure royal prerogatives to sidestep anti-Catholic laws and appoint fellow religionists to important positions in the army, local government and the universities. When such action was challenged in the courts, as in the Godden v. Hales case of 1686, the King put his right to appoint and dismiss judges to good effect. The ill-planned rebellion of Charles II's Protestant illegitimate son, the Duke of Monmouth, was swiftly crushed and James stationed a powerful standing army on Hounslow Heath to overawe London. As steps were taken to arrange parliamentary elections to ensure a House of Commons favourable to James's plans, it looked for a while as if England might become an absolute Catholic state along French lines.

The coronation of James II in Westminster Abbey.

Charles II's illegitimate son, the Duke of Monmouth, attempted to seize the throne in 1685, but was defeated at the Battle of Sedgemoor.

However, when a trial of the Archbishop of Canterbury and other bishops collapsed, and the birth of a male heir gave rise to the spectre of a line of Catholic kings, the loyalty of the political nation, both Whig and Tory, would stretch no further. A request for help went out to the husband of James's Protestant daughter, Mary. It began: 'The people are ... generally dissatisfied with the present conduct of the government in relation to their religion, liberties and properties (all of which have been greatly invaded).' In November 1688 William of Orange landed at Torbay. Within a few weeks James found himself without support, and he fled to France. After some argument William and Mary were accepted as joint sovereigns. (This event was to be known as the Glorious Revolution.)

A new constitution was founded in the Bill of Rights (1689), a Toleration Act (1689), a Triennial Act (1694) and the Act of Settlement (1701). Parliament was given a permanent and vital part in the government, controlling all taxation and the armed forces. The law courts were freed from political interference, dissenters were permitted to worship as they wished and future monarchs were to be members of the Protestant Church of England.

William and Mary

William of Orange, who became William III in 1689, was not an attractive man. Bishop Burnet described him as of 'a thin and weak body', 'always asthmatical' with 'a constant deep cough'. Moreover he had 'a coldness in his way that damps a modest man extremely, for he hears things with a dry silence that shows too much of distrust of those to whom he speaks.' William was never popular in England, for it was felt that he had acquired the throne through his wife, and after the death of the tall and attractive Mary in December 1694 William's position was even more difficult. Nevertheless, the English nation owed William a great deal.

William III and Mary II reigned as joint sovereigns, although after Mary's death in 1694 there was some resentment felt towards William.

William III presiding over a meeting of both the Lords and Commons at Parliament in 1689.

In the ten years previous to William's accession political parties had started to emerge: the Tories were loyal to the Church of England and traditional royal prerogatives, while the Whigs were suspicious of royal power, seeking to limit it with parliamentary authority. They attracted Dissenting followers. The principles behind the 1688–9 revolution were Whig, but William obviously felt more secure with the loyalist Tories, although he wished to rule without the exclusive support of any party or group. A further problem for William was that the Whigs were more ready to support him in his war with Louis XIV.

When they turned to William for help, the English knew that they were involving themselves in European war – that was the price of William's aid. Indeed, he never really liked England but accepted the crown to ensure her help for his beloved Holland. Although his armies were successful against James II and the Anglo-Dutch fleets controlled the seas, on land the long-drawn out war of seiges usually went Louis's way. William's one great victory was the recapture of the fortress of Namur in 1695.

The effects of the war at home were dramatic. In order to pay for it Parliament agreed to an unprecedented 20 per cent land tax. The National Debt (1693) and the Bank of England (1694) were founded and the coinage was re-minted. To enable this 'financial revolution' to work, Parliament became a semi-permanent institution (elections were held every three years) without whose support no government could hope to operate. The English revolution was complete.

Anne

Until recently Anne (1702–14) has not received her just deserts in the pages of history books. She was smitten with a dull husband and the personal tragedy, despite 18 pregnancies, of seeing all her children die before they reached adulthood. Understandably, she assumed ample proportions in later life, but her physical heaviness was not matched by any bluntness of wit or perception.

Anne inherited the tricky political situation which had exasperated William. Parliament was only gradually discovering ways of working as the major political power in the land, and the unstable parties added to the confusion. At first the queen relied upon non-party men, John Churchill (Duke of Marlborough and Captain General of the Forces), Lord Godolphin (Lord Treasurer, 1702–10) and Robert Harley (Speaker of the House of Commons, 1702–4; Secretary of State, 1704–8). The war against France, known as the War of Spanish

Queen Anne (1702–14), the last of the Stuart monarchs, exerted a steadying influence on the heady politics of the age.

The French were defeated by John Churchill at the Battle of Blenheim in 1704.

Succession since one of its aims was to settle the successor to the massive Spanish empire, went well for England and her allies (Holland, the Holy Roman Empire and several German states). Marlborough inflicted the first ever serious defeat on Louis XIV near Blenheim in Austria in 1704. He wrote hastily home to his wife Sarah, 'I have not time to say more but to beg that you will give my duty to the Queen, and let her know her army has had a glorious victory.'

Blenheim was followed with further victories at Ramillies (1706), Oudenarde (1708) and Malplaquet, on French soil (1709). But by now the Tories were building strong opposition to the high taxation that the campaigns demanded, and following riots at the government's attempted prosecution of a Tory parson, Henry Sacheverell, Anne dismissed Godolphin in 1710, then Marlborough in 1711. The Tories, led by Harley (now Earl of Oxford) and Viscount Bolingbroke, were in power.

The 1701 Act of Settlement had stated that if Anne died without leaving an heir, the English throne was to pass to the nearest Protestant claimant, the children of Sophia of Hanover who was descended from a daughter of James I. Fearing an end to their power if this came about, the leading Tories began to approach the son of James II, a Catholic member of the House of Stuart. Five days before her death, however, Anne dismissed the Tories, clearing the path for the Hanoverian succession and the end of the Stuart Age.

7 A CHANGING NATION

Christopher Hill, the great historian of the seventeenth century, entitled his book on the Stuart era *The Century of Revolution*. Subsequently historians have argued about the nature of that revolution and its exact timing, but few disagree that the extent and swiftness of the changes which took place during the seventeenth century were indeed little short of revolutionary. The England of 1714 was in many ways unrecognizable from that of 1603.

The standard of living

One of the earliest detailed breakdowns of English society is left for us by Gregory King (1648–1712). In 1697 he presented the Board of Trade with a remarkable work entitled 'Natural and Political Observations and Conclusions upon the State and Condition of England'. He estimated the population of the country to be $5\frac{1}{2}$ million. By 1714 the population had probably risen further, to perhaps $5\frac{3}{4}$ million, an increase over the century of almost two million.

In Stuart times Manchester was just beginning to emerge as an industrial centre.

The South West Prospect of Manchester and Salford

For the poor, a good or bad harvest was a matter of life or death in the Stuart Age.

The rise in population was not uniform. Towns had grown rapidly, accounting for almost 18 per cent of the population by 1714. London, as always, led the way with over half a million inhabitants, but some of the great cities of the industrial revolution were also beginning to emerge: Birmingham (7,500) and Manchester (13,000) in particular.

From the middle of the century onwards prices were steady and agricultural output rose, enabling the new mouths to be fed and a slight increase in the overall standard of living to take place. It is estimated that in the early seventeenth century wheat fields yielded eleven bushels an acre, while by 1700 this had almost doubled to twenty bushels. Thus John Houghton wrote in 1682, '. . . since His Majesty's most happy Restoration the whole land hath been fermented and stirred up by the profitable hints it hath received from the Royal Society by which means . . . the rent of the kingdom is far greater than ever it was.'

The Royal Society was founded in 1660 to promote scientific and technological education and experiment, and the sort of 'profitable hints' which it and other sources offered to farmers can be put in two categories. Firstly, farmers were encouraged to enclose their fields and rotate their crops, to maintain the fertility of the soil. This was supported with new crops (such as turnips), drainage and better hoeing. Secondly, farmers began to specialize, producing what their region grew best. When George I came to the throne he inherited a country whose agriculture was about the most up-to-date in the western world.

The Royal Society, here shown in session, was founded in 1660 and played a major part in encouraging the advancement of science.

Economic development

'New discoveries in metals, mines and minerals, new undertakings in trade, engines, manufactures, in a nation pushing and improving as we are: these things open new scenes every day, and make England especially show a new and differing face in many places, on every occasion of surveying it.' Thus wrote Daniel Defoe shortly after the close of the Stuart era. He was fully aware, as were most contemporaries, that after about 1650 England's economy had begun spectacular development.

There were two aspects to this development: a diversification and sophistication of domestic manufacture, and a rapid and sustained growth of overseas trade, helped by a more effective banking, credit and insurance system. Woollen cloth still accounted for about 65 per cent of English exports by 1714, but the range of goods had grown and the mining and metallurgical industries (coal, iron, tin, copper, lead) were now eating away at wool's near-monopoly. Thomas Newcomen's steam mine pump (1708) and Abraham Darby's method of smelting iron with coke rather than wood (1709–10) were both of much future significance.

Shipbuilding, requiring a whole range of skilled trades and specialized manufactures, was one of the country's most vital developing industries.

The expansion in overseas trade, helped by Navigation Acts that ordered that all goods traded with England or her colonies be carried in English ships, at this time amounted to a veritable 'commercial revolution'. From the colonies came sugar, tobacco, tea, coffee and chocolate, much of which was re-exported to Europe. In the New World many of these goods were produced by slave labour, and the transport of slaves from West Africa was another key feature of English trade at this time.

It is estimated that in six early years of the reign of Charles II England's imports, valued at £4,400,000, exceeded her exports by £300,000. By the 1720s the situation had been dramatically reversed: between 1722 and 1724 exports (worth a total of £7,750,000) exceeded imports by £1 million. England was becoming the commercial centre of the world.

During the Stuart Age English farming made considerable advances, as farmers began to employ new scientific methods.

By the end of the seventeenth century shipbuilding had become a major British industry.

New wealth

Even so, by the end of the Stuart Age the majority of Englishmen and women still lived in poverty. Gregory King estimated that 2,675,520 people increased the wealth of the kingdom, while a slightly larger number decreased it because they were frequently dependent upon charity. Nevertheless, there is some evidence that there was a slight rise in living standards for the whole population during the reigns of the last four Stuarts, while there is plenty more evidence that for the growing number of 'producers' (farmers, merchants, landlords and shippers for example) there was definitely more money in circulation.

The new wealth of the fortunate found expression in numerous ways. Splendid houses were constructed both in the town and country, using the beautiful proportions pioneered by classical architects. Coffee, chocolate and tea houses sprang up and the consumption of tobacco multiplied to 13 million lb by 1700. Some expressed their wealth in very ostentatious ways, such as the young man described in 1700: 'His cravat reached down to his middle and had stuff enough in it to make a sail for a barge. A most prodigious cravat-string peeped from under his chin, the two corners of which in conjunction with a monstrous periwig that would have made a Laplander sweat under the North Pole, eclipsed three-quarters of his face.'

Not all expenditure was vulgar. The age saw a flourishing of publishing, furniture making, painting and crafts of every kind. Indeed, it is possible to see in the early eighteenth century, at least for a limited section of the population, the emergence of a consumer society.

Wealthy men enjoyed dressing in ostentatious clothes and wearing 'monstrous periwigs'.

Coffee houses were the popular haunts of the fashionable in the early eighteenth century.

8 LAW, LEISURE AND THE FAMILY

Despite its beautiful works of art, its outstanding literature, fine buildings and commercial progress, the seventeenth century was a rough age in which anyone returning from the twentieth century would feel frighteningly out of place. Cruelty to both man and beast was widespread, as were disease, disfigurement and death. The treatment of women and children was unfair and, at worst, disgraceful. Simple comforts which we take for granted, such as running hot water, were totally absent. Society was riven with snobbery: without thinking, seventeenth century men and women divided each other into rigid social groups.

Society was structured into rigid class divisions. Here the lord of the manor instructs his tenants and their families.

High society

In 1696 Gregory King estimated there to be 15,000 gentlemen and Esquires in England, above whom on the social scale were a mere 1,500 Knights and Lords. This 2 per cent of the population owned perhaps 65 per cent of the land, from which most of their wealth came. Not many of the aristocracy could trace their ancestry back beyond the Tudor era but nonetheless they jealously guarded their privileged position in society.

The wealthier families had seats in the country and houses in London, perhaps in the areas being developed at the west end of the city. In their counties these families carried tremendous influence, which, in the first half of the century at least, rivalled the king's powers. This power was based upon the fact that they controlled the local offices, such as Lord Lieutenant and Justice of the Peace, and many local farmers were their tenants, with little security of tenure.

The households of the rich were run by an army of servants, including gardeners, grooms, coachmen, stable lads, kitchen maids, footmen, ladies' maids and so forth. The ladies of the family were legally disadvantaged compared with the men and it was inconceivable for them to undertake any form of job. Women were expected to be fair and delicate, hence the appeal of this advertisement of 1702: 'The Venetian Wash, being a Most Excellent Water, to beautify and add loveliness to the face, by taking out all sorts of freckles, sun-brown and yellowness. 1s the Bottle.' Today most of us regard a tan as beautiful! Ladies were expected to manage the household, however, and that in itself, could be a full-time occupation. Seventeenth-century children were often seen as being in need of harsh discipline to make them civilized Christians. They were dressed in smaller versions of adult clothing, given a harsh classics-based education, and subjected to severe punishment. By the end of the Stuart era this was starting to change: in the more enlightened homes both women and children were being treated much more humanely, as people in their own right.

The common people

Beneath the glittering society of the peerage and gentlefolk stretched the mass of the population. They ranged from the prosperous merchants, lawyers and office holders (of whom Gregory King estimated there to be about 29,000) to millions of labourers, servants, paupers and vagrants. The middle classes aped their social superiors in life style, but for the poor the business of scraping together a living needed all their energies.

The dwelling of an agricultural labourer would be a simple, thatched cottage of one or two rooms, without sanitation, water and probably without even glass in the windows. Diet would depend on the season

A typical London scene in late Stuart times. Notice how the child is dressed as a miniature adult.

and the harvest. After a prosperous year or two the poor, especially in the latter half of the century, would have sufficient to live on, but in times of hardship they literally starved. During the wars against France and Spain in the reign of Charles I some discharged Irish soldiers were found near the coast eating grass to keep themselves alive.

For the poor there was no education, and no proper medical services. The hours of work, as set out by the magistrates of Warwick in 1684, were from 5 am to 8 pm, with $2\frac{1}{2}$ hours free for meals, sleep and 'drinkings'. The pay for a labourer was 1s (5p) a day. It is not surprising that the English philosopher John Locke commented of poor children, 'What they can have at home from their parents is seldom more than bread and water, and that very scantily too.'

Two lawyers present their cases before a judge. Until 1689, judges were appointed and dismissed by the king.

Judge Jeffreys (1648–89), one of a group of Stuart judges notorious for their harsh sentences.

The law

At the opening of the Stuart era there were three legal systems in the land, the common (or traditional) law courts, the royal prerogative courts and the Church courts. Prerogative courts, the most famous of which was the Star Chamber, had developed gradually in the past to offer swifter, cheaper and fairer justice than that of the common law. But as the seventeenth century progressed they became disliked for the arbitrary way they upheld royal authority. As a result of this almost all the prerogative courts were abolished in 1641.

Until the Glorious Revolution of 1688 judges were royal appointments who could be dismissed if they offended the king in their judgements. Throughout the period the courts of England were bullied and hectored by a number of judges noted for their harshness. None was more notorious than Judge Jeffreys who vigorously pursued the Duke of Monmouth's defeated rebel army in 1685: '... his delights were, accordingly, drinking, laughing, singing, kissing, as all the extravagances of the bottle ... his weakness was that he could not reprehend without scolding; and in such Billingsgate language as should come out of the mouth of any man.' Billingsgate was the London fish market, famous for its foul smells and even fouler language!

The law was established and guarded by the upper classes and seen by them very much as a protection against the possible insurrection of the lower orders. Punishments were, therefore, very severe, particularly for behaviour that led to riot or theft of property. Execution and torture were relatively common in an age which held life so cheap.

Leisure

The life of seventeenth-century men and women should not be viewed through too gloomy a glass. We regard with horror their suffering, forgetting that they knew no different. Their lives were shorter than ours, but perhaps more vigorous, and people threw themselves into their entertainment more energetically than we do today.

Hunting was the sport of the court and upper classes. James I was devoted to it and was criticized for the amount of time he spent in the saddle chasing deer and boars rather than attending to the business of state. Charles II preferred horse racing to hunting. He also took an interest in yachting. Indoors the rich played cards, listened (often inattentively) to music, attended plays, danced and drank. Indeed, drinking, often to excess, was the most popular leisure-time pursuit of all social classes.

Although there were few organized team games, the English were very keen on individual athletic pursuits, such as real tennis, running, wrestling, boxing, leaping and tossing the pike. Less energetic but equally popular were shooting (with guns or bows), bowls, falconry and angling. Duelling was forbidden, but not uncommon.

The aspect of seventeenth-century entertainment that we find most difficult to appreciate or understand is the delight in the torture of animals. Cock fighting was common, but the greatest thrill was baiting bulls or bears with dogs, leading to a fight to the death between the two: 'First a young ox or bull was led in and fastened by a long rope to an iron ring in the middle of the yard; then about thirty dogs, two or three at a time, were let loose on him, but he made short work of them, goring them and tossing them high in the air ... Several had such a grip of the bull's throat or ear that their mouths had to be forced open with poles.'

James I neglected affairs of state on many occasions in order to enjoy the pleasures of the chase.

9 THE ARTS

The seventeenth century was one of the most creative in the history of English arts. It encompasses the finest plays of Shakespeare, the architectural genius of Sir Christopher Wren, and the outstanding musical skills of Henry Purcell.

The Renaissance
Growing from roots in late-medieval Italy, in early modern Europe a revival of interest in all things classical took place. This was coupled with greater emphasis upon the individual in this life as opposed to the hereafter. In Italy the sweeping cultural and intellectual change, known as the Renaissance, was led by the artistic genius of men such as Leonardo da Vinci (1452–1519) and Michaelangelo (1475–1564); but it was not for another sixty years at least that the movement was adopted and adapted by English artists. Nowhere is this more apparent than in the field of architecture.

The Banqueting Hall in Whitehall Palace, built by Inigo Jones for James I. Charles I stepped from one of its windows on to the scaffold in 1649.

St Paul's Cathedral, rebuilt by Sir Christopher Wren after the fire of London (1666), remains one of the city's finest buildings.

The architect who first introduced the true rules of classical proportion to English building was Inigo Jones (1573–1652), Surveyor General of the King's Works from 1615, and designer of such clean classical buildings as the Queen's House at Greenwich and the Banqueting Hall in Whitehall, from a window of which Charles I stepped to his execution in 1649.

Although Jones's work is appealing, it required the genius of Christopher Wren (1632–1723) to adapt the fine lines and pure form of classicism to a native style of building. The great fire of London in 1666 gave him, as Surveyor General, the opportunity to design and build the fine new St Paul's Cathedral and 52 other churches. On a less grand scale the influence of men such as Jones and Wren made itself felt not only in the country houses that sprang up all over England in the later seventeenth and eighteenth centuries, but also in the neat, beautifully proportioned town houses that are such an attractive legacy of the period.

Education

The great majority of seventeenth-century children received little or no formal education. It has been suggested that in 1642 more than 70 per cent of the adult male population were illiterate. In fact literacy and prosperity usually went hand in hand. In many towns there were grammar schools, originally founded for all local children, but by the seventeenth century the local gentry all but monopolized their use. The situation pertains to this day, for many of these grammar schools are now the independent public schools.

Among the better-off the late sixteenth and early seventeenth centuries witnessed a quite remarkable flowering of formal education. In the 1590s the yeomen of Leicestershire were 77 per cent illiterate, a figure which had fallen to 55 per cent by the 1640s, by which time virtually all the gentry could read and write fluently. It became increasingly common for those who could afford it to attend, at least for a while, university (Oxford or Cambridge) and one of the Inns of Court. This was often followed by a 'finishing journey' abroad, in which the young gentleman was escorted round western Europe by a tutor.

Oxford was the Royalist headquarters for most of the Civil War and remained a centre of traditional support for much of the century.

M^R· W I L L I A M
SHAKESPEAR'S

Comedies, Histories, and Tragedies.

Published according to the true Original Copies.

The third Impression.

And unto this Impression is added seven Playes, never
before Printed in Folio.

viz.

Pericles Prince of *Tyre.*
The *London Prodigall.*
The History of *Thomas* Ld. *Cromwell.*
Sir *John Oldcastle* Lord *Cobham.*
The *Puritan Widow.*
A *York-shire* Tragedy.
The Tragedy of *Locrine.*

*By the middle of the seventeenth century, when this edition of his works
was published, Shakespeare's pre-eminent place in literature was firmly
established.*

Hours at school were long and punishment severe. Pupils were often
expected to converse in nothing but Latin, for the classics lay at the
heart of the curriculum. The more fortunate were educated at home by
a tutor. For girls the opportunities for a good education were much
more remote. There were girls' boarding schools but, in the opinion of
one hostile contemporary at least, they were not very good; the girls
merely 'learn to quaver instead of singing, hop for dancing ... and
scratch and thumb the lute. To conclude, they learn nothing more
gentle, but only to be so gentle that they commonly run away with the
first serving-man or younger brother who makes love to them.'

Literature and art

There is no way that one can do justice in a few paragraphs to the magnificence of the literature produced during the Stuart age. Although plays were banned during the interregnum, the vigorous heritage of Shakespeare (1564–1616) and Ben Jonson (1573–1637) was taken up and given new form by the so-called Restoration dramatists, foremost among whom are William Wycherley (1640–1716), William Congreve (1670 – 1729) and Sir John Vanbrugh (1664–1726). In poetry the century is no less rich. The biting satirical skill of John Dryden (1631–1700) at the end of the century provides an exciting balance to the rich cadences of John Milton's (1608–1674) epic *Paradise Lost* and the poignant perfection of Shakespeare's sonnets.

In prose the century showed perhaps the most striking literary development. The heavy, learned style of the Tudors was gradually refined and sharpened, a process helped by the outpouring of pamphlets at the time of the civil war. By the early eighteenth century newspapers were a regular feature of the life of the capital and other large towns, and in the hands of men like Daniel Defoe (1660–1731, the author of *Robinson Crusoe* and *Moll Flanders*) the modern novel was being created.

In the world of art English painters are dwarfed by the Dutchman Van Dyck who worked extensively for Charles I. Later in the century Sir Godfrey Kneller (1646–1723) produced skilful portraits, but it is not until the eighteenth century that English art really established its own identity. The same is not true of music. There had always been a strong native tradition of composition, from the Tudor genius of Thomas Tallis (1505–1585) through the madrigal composers William Byrd (1542–1623) and Thomas Morley (1557–1603), and which merged with current continental fashions in the varied work of Henry Purcell (1658–1695).

It is in its arts that the Stuart age is most readily accessible to us. Like the century itself, we are left with an impression of vigorous diversity and development. Nowhere is the pride of the emerging nation more apparent than in the vastness of Blenheim Palace, given by a grateful nation to the Duke of Marlborough for his victories over the French. Yet it is probably in the secret, personal diary of a civil servant, not in any of the great public creations, that we come closest to the spirit of the age. And as we read Samuel Pepys (1633–1703) we realize that, despite the considerable changes which have taken place since his time, the men and women of Stuart England were really very little different from ourselves:

Left Robinson Crusoe *by Daniel Defoe was based upon the real-life adventures of Alexander Selkirk.*

Samuel Pepys, whose diaries, as well as being a delight to read, tell us more than any other single source about the life of our Stuart predecessors.

'11 June, 1665 . . . In the evening comes Mr. Andrews and his wife, and Mr. Hill, and stayed and played and sung and supped—most excellent pretty company; so pleasant, ingenious, and harmless, I cannot desire better. They gone, we to bed—my mind in great present ease.'

DATE CHART

1603	Accession of James I
1605	Gunpowder plot
	Shakespeare's *King Lear* first performed
1607	Jamestown Colony founded in America
1610	Failure of the Great Contract, a proposed financial deal by which James I would surrender certain rights in return for a regular supply of money from Parliament
1611	Authorized Version of the Bible published
1614	Addled Parliament
1620	Voyage of the *Mayflower* to New World
1625	Accession of Charles I
	War with Spain
1627	War with France
1628	Petition of Right accepted by Charles I
	Harvey's work on the circulation of the blood published
1629	Charles I begins period of rule without Parliament
1632	Thomas Wentworth becomes Lord Deputy in Ireland
	William Laud becomes Archbishop of Canterbury
	The Court of Star Chamber orders the ears of the Puritan pamphleteer, William Prynne, to be cut off
1637	East India Company sets up bases in China
1638	Scottish rebellion begins
1640	Long Parliament meets
1642	Civil War begins
1644	Royalist forces defeated at Marston Moor
1645	Charles I surrenders to the Scots
1649	Charles I executed
	England becomes a republic
1650	Tea first drunk in England
1651	Navigation Acts to protect English shipping passed
1652–4	First Anglo–Dutch war
1653	Cromwell becomes Lord Protector
1658	Cromwell dies
1660	Pepys begins his diary
	Charles II restored
1661–5	Clarendon Code limits rights of dissenters
1664–7	Second Anglo–Dutch war
	English capture New Amsterdam (renamed New York)
1665	Last serious plague in London

1666	Great fire of London	**1694**	Bank of England founded
1667	Milton's *Paradise Lost* published	**1700**	Congreve's *The Way of the World* first performed
1672–4	Third Anglo–Dutch war		
1675	Wycherley's *The Country Wife* first performed and published	**1701**	Act of Settlement confirms the Protestant succession
1678	Bunyan's *The Pilgrim's Progress* published	**1702**	Accession of Anne War of Spanish Succession First English daily newspaper published
1681	Charles II defeats the Whig efforts to exclude the Duke of York from the throne Dryden's *Absolem and Achitophel* published	**1704**	Gibraltar captured by English fleet Battle of Blenheim
1685	Accession of James II	**1707**	Act of Union of Scotland and England
1687	Newton's *Principia Mathematica* published	**1709**	Darby uses coke to smelt iron ore
1688	James II flees	**1710**	Tories come to power St Paul's Cathedral completed
1689	Throne declared vacant and offered jointly to William III and Mary II Bill of Rights Toleration Act Purcell's *Dido and Aeneas* written	**1711**	The *Spectator* founded by Joseph Addison
1690	Turnips first grown in England	**1712**	Pope's *The Rape of the Lock* published Last execution for witchcraft
1692	Lloyd's coffee house opened as centre of the marine insurance business	**1713**	Treaty of Utrecht ends War of Spanish Succession
		1714	Accession of George I

GLOSSARY

Absolute With total power.
Anglican Pertaining to the Church of England.
Anarchy The absence of regular government.
Arbitrary Bound by no rules or constitution.
Burgess A wealthy citizen.
Customs Duty paid on goods entering or leaving the country.
Dissenter A member of a Protestant sect outside the Church of England.
Enlightened Broad-minded and up-to-date.
Exclusion The policy of keeping the Catholic James Duke of York from the English throne.
Faction A political group seeking favour and reward at court.
Hierarchy Established order.
Inns of Court The London legal societies responsible for admitting barristers to practice.
Interregnum The gap between two reigns.
Madrigal A light song sung in parts.
Magistrate A Justice of the Peace.
Malnutrition Undernourishment.
Militia The county amateur defence force.
Monopoly Sole exclusive control over a trade or manufacture.
Nonconformist A member of a Protestant sect outside the Church of England.
Pagan Non-Christian.
Prerogative Royal powers and privileges.
Profligate Spendthrift, wastrel.
Reformation The period that saw the division of the Church between Catholic and Protestant.
Republic A country without a monarchy.
Subject One who owes obedience to a king or queen.
Tenant One paying rent for land or a house.
Tories Supporters of the traditional royal prerogative, the Anglican Church and English withdrawal from entanglement in European war and politics.
Vagrant A homeless wanderer.
Vernacular The langauge of one's native country.
Whigs Supporters of policies to limit royal power, further religious toleration and of an aggressive foreign policy.
Yeoman An independent small farmer.

FURTHER READING

General surveys
Coward, B. *The Stuart Age*, (Longman, 1980)
Jones, J. R. *Country and Court 1658–1714* (Arnold, 1978)
Roots, I. *The Great Rebellion 1640–1660* (Batsford, 1966)
Also recommended are the volumes in Macmillan's *Problems in Focus* series, and the volumes in Longman's *Seminar Studies* series

Society, religion and politics
Coleman, D. C. *The Economy of England 1450–1750* (London, 1977)
Morrill, J. *The Revolt of the Provinces* (Longman, 1980)
Thomas, K. *Religion and the Decline of Magic* (Weidenfeld & Nicolson, 1971)

Biography
Ashley, M. *Cromwell and Charles I* (Methuen, 1987)
Fraser, A. *Charles II* (Futura, 1981)
Gregg, E. P. *Queen Anne* (Routledge, 1980)
Willson, D. H. *James VI and I* (Cape, 1963)

Contemporary sources
Aubrey, J. *Brief Lives* (various editions)
Burnet, G. *A History of His Own Time* (Everyman, 1979)
Latham, R. (Ed.) *The Shorter Pepys* (Bell & Hyman, 1985)
The Oxford Book of Seventeenth Century Verse (Oxford University Press, 1934)

PICTURE ACKNOWLEDGEMENTS

The illustrations were supplied by BBC Hulton Picture Library 13, 17, 26, 34, 44, 49, 54, 55, 65, 66, 67, 69; e. t. archive *cover*; Mary Evans Picture Library 8, 9, 10, 11, 12, 14, 18, 24, 25, 28, 30, 31, 32, 33, 35, 36, 37, 39, 40, 41, 42, 43, 48, 51, 52, 53, 56, 57, 58, 59, 61, 62, 68, 70, 72. All other pictures were supplied by the Wayland Picture Library.

INDEX

Jones, Inigo 67
Jonson, Ben 71

Kneller, Sir Godfrey 71

Laud, William, Archbishop 21,
    31–2, 38
Law, the 11, 15, 63
Leisure pursuits 64
Life expectancy 10
Literature 71
Local government 15, 46, 60
Long Parliament (the Rump) 21,
    23
Louis XIV 27, 45, 49

Milton, John 29, 71

Navigation Acts 55
New Model Army 24, 40
New World, the 42, 44, 55
Newton, Sir Isaac 37

Old Pretender, the 38
Overseas trade 55

Parliament 15, 16, 20
Pepys, Samuel 71–2
Petition of Right 20
Political nation 15, 16, 18, 26, 45,
    47
Population 9, 10, 12, 52, 60
Poverty 56, 62
Privy Council, the 16
Protestantism 17, 29
Purcell, Henry 66

Puritans 17, 23, 31–2

Reformation, the 29, 36
Religious toleration 25, 36
Renaissance, the 66
Restoration dramatists 71
Restoration, the 38
Royal Society, the 53

Science 10, 37
Scotland 21
    union with England 38
Shakespeare, William 66, 71
Slavery 55
Spain 42
Star Chamber, the 63

Taxation 27, 49
Tenant farmers 60
Toleration Act, 1689 32, 36,
    37
Tories 27, 47, 49, 51

Van Dyck, Sir Anthony 71
Verney, Sir Edmund 23

Wars
    with the Dutch 27, 43
    of Spanish Succession 50
Wentworth, Thomas, Earl of
    Strafford 21, 40
Whigs 27, 41, 49
William III 41, 43
    and Mary 47–8
Women, position of 11, 60
Wren, Sir Christopher 66–7